EVERYTHING
- that makes my -
NANA
SPECIAL
what I Love About You...

~ contents ~

1. Gratitude
2. Love
3. Fun
4. Letter to Nana

Written By...

THANK YOU, NANA!

1. Gratitude

Three reasons I'm GRATEFUL for you...

1. _____

2. _____

3. _____

NANA, THANK YOU for TEACHING me how to...

_____

Thank you for ALWAYS...

_____

and helping me...

. . . .

THANK YOU for giving me...

_____

and PLAYING...

....

with me.

My FAVORITE thing to do with you is...

_____

Your hugs ALWAYS...

_____

{ You make me SMILE when you... }

_____

Nana, you are...

_____
(one word to describe Nana)

Three things you're REALLY good at...

1. _____

2. _____

3. _____

Nana, you have the very BEST...

_____

My favorite memory with you was the time we...

_____

_____

because...

. . . .

I know you LOVE me when you...

{ Nana, I feel the happiest when we... }

_____

together.

You make ME feel SUPER special when you...

> I love EATING...

_____

with you.

NANA, if you were a FLOWER, you would be...

_____

because...

. . . .

You're smarter than...

~ coupons for Nana ~
Mark the box after using each coupon!

~ Finish the book by writing a short letter to Nana ~

To Nana...

_____

_____

_____

_____

Love From _____

Made in United States
Troutdale, OR
03/03/2025

29493543R00024